Deep Shadow and Winter's Dark

by
Alexander J. Cunningham

Published by Frontier Writers Publishing 2012

Artwork by
Gail Curran 2012

ISBN 978-1-906306-17-5

Published by Frontier Writers Publishing 2012

Introduction

This book in your hands, *Deep Shadow and Winter's Dark,* is a collection of 111 Haiku/Senryu style poems.

They are a mix of inspired, imagined and, in no small way, provoked verses written in the span of a year.

As with the collection, *Beautiful but with Thorns,* which preceded this book, the verses centre on relationships, with all of their beginnings, endings and the fleeting moments in-between.

Whether you're in Love or in Hate, there is certain to be a verse here for you.

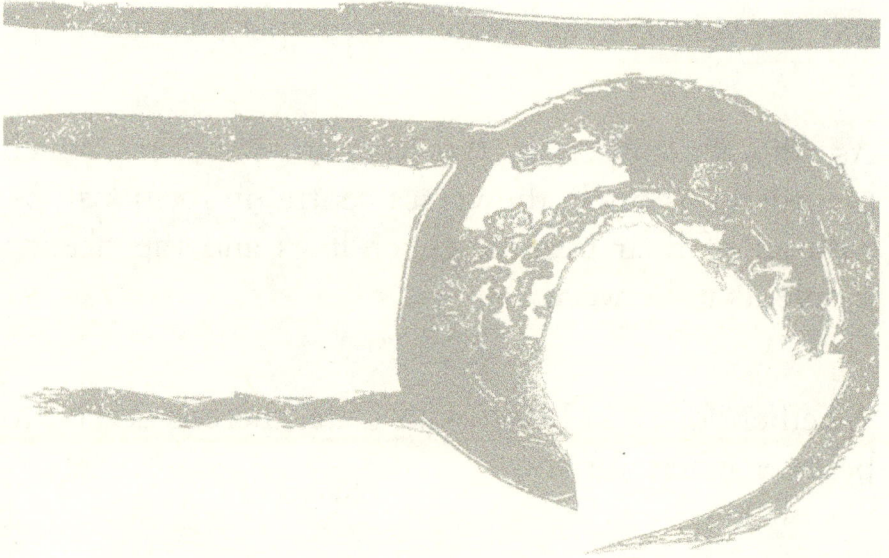

walking through the gallery

our life imitates art:

The Kiss.

time stops-

the world falls silent

when your lips touch mine

time without clocks

travel without conditions

and a future free to shape

while with you

summer sun shines

all the brighter

with her in my arms

I need want for nothing-

heart's desire

crumpled on the floor

your Little Black Dress

shed in passion

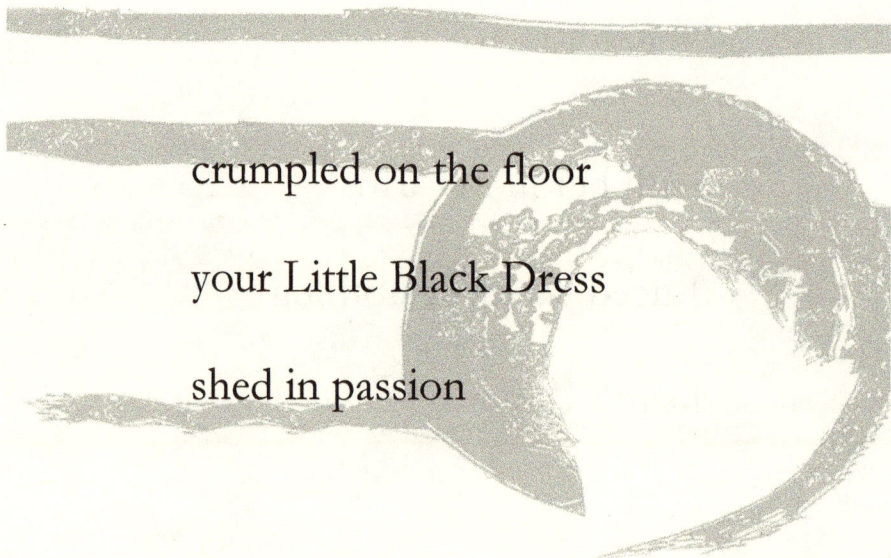

wrapped in each others arms

songs on the radio

speak to our hearts and minds

diamonds rolling from your eyes

priceless-

our fate in Your hands

your bright heart

fills my world-

light in a dark place

unlooked for but not unwelcome

your precious cargo-

true collaborative creation

wrists bound by silk

heart bound by Love-

your dominion over me absolute

my arms encircle your body

drawing you close to me-

our hearts beat as one

in dreams I kiss you-

awake

I wish for dreams

evening becomes night

as you sleep in my arms-

will we ever see the dawn?

curled in my bed

you dream in purring repose-

this too shall pass

without you beside me

all I have is my fear

you won't return

hanging on her promises

bound to her every desire-

this fool's a fool for love

without you in my arms

all I can hold are memories-

the ghost of your touch

borne in the heart of passion

yet cooled in waters of contemplation-

tempered love is made adamant

crisp golden leaf

lands in my lap-

autumn's first victim

between loss and love

a void

only self can fill

sackcloth and ashes

infant's blood for blusher-

"It's a good look for you, love."

shifting Summer sun bathes

an empty hospital bed-

free to be at peace

staring into your eyes

trying to recognise who I once knew-

naught but a stranger

Exhibit A: one crumpled photo

uncovered in the clearout-

Inexplicable **E**motional **D**amage

with distance between us again

I'm left with your image

and the memories we made together

our good times-

if only I could remember them

without sorrow's long shadow

ghosts of His old lovers

haunt Her mind-

"Has he done this with them?"

fading sun foreshadows

winter's growing darkness-

dwell in sleepless nights

wishes upon falling stars

only grant what one deserves-

celestial bodies turn to ash

conjoined lovers heart

once beat for both-

soul survivor

beer can pyramids

upon a pizzabox plateau-

the architecture of angst

checking out the talent-

wedding ring

tucked in his pocket

seeking faith in others

while denying ones own lack-

self-indulgent hypocrisy

one short lifetime-

room for mistakes

but not forever

institutionalised by law

freedom is feared

until one can accept change-

oft heard tales

of what once was-

too rich for my blood

to forgive and not forget

is to be cut and healed-

there's always a scar

deities in the details-

spare me those moments

where **U** and **I** ain't **Us**

hollowed out heart-

he tries to fill the void

without lies and pain

a man without a wife

like a flagellant without a whip-

happier than he'll admit

making friends with lovers

no easy task-

green eyed monster

on the road

from ruins of the past-

salt the earth

only remembering the good times

a fatal flaw-

endings don't arrive alone

bought with love

worn through time-

the solitaire passes on

between love and loss

a lesson for the heart-

will I ever learn?

with provenance altered

she wears my gift-

friendship rings true

free for the future

yet burdened by the past-

I move through a present imperfect

"you and no other"-

words on silver bands

which never came to pass

sacrificing our **All** for our **Other**-

what little remains

is a mere ending

poetic license grants anonymity

shrouding misfortune in verse-

attraction knows no falsehood

woodsmoke on the chill air

first scent of autumn-

long shadows fall

vacant at visiting time

plastic chairs disappear-

solitary sleepless confinement

white falls through black

tears in Winter's chill-

sorrow best served cold

deserted roads and darkened windows-

negative images of mind and heart

for this insomniac's dog walk

my Christmas list has grown

yet what gift can go unnoticed?-

not even my love

cold crimson cruelty

spills from the heart-

black in Winter's night

with the divine unmasked

a truth is unveiled-

false deities & hollow worship

hospital disinfectant stings

cold and sneezing noses-

snarling snowbound psyche

nocturnal hours-

habitat for the loveless

and those left betrayed

footprints on wet sand.

a sign of our journey together-

high tide drowns all trace

acting on a whim

staging a set up-

theatre of love as war

old songs gain

brand new meaning-

"Why didn't I see it before?"

this season of separations

force change unrelenting-

what Truths may survive?

our sweat-sheened bodies

locked

in a breathless embrace

as my heartbeat slows-skin cooling

the heat of desire

stirs within me once again

and with a kiss

cupping your face in my hands

we begin again

light at the end of the tunnel-

soon I will emerge

blinking at freedom's radiance

witnessed through drifting flakes

in nocturnal shades of white-

my red petaled gift to you

revelations sow seeds

growing choking weeds-

bitter black fruit

late Summer sun

lights up her face-

better late than never

love letter lies

awaiting my return-

proof of life after you

memories of childhood Summers

blazing sun baking the earth-

canyons for spiders

out of reach

except in my dreams

I hold you – kiss you

placing brush to canvas

I describe my love for you-

scarlet and shades of Payne's Grey

deep shadow and Winter's dark-

friends to illicit lovers

sharing a moment of passion

your image in my mind

brings you closer-

rest within my heart

sunlit Winter woodland walk

then curled up in our bed-

in my (day)dreams

Christmas gone

a New Year beckons

with you at it's heart

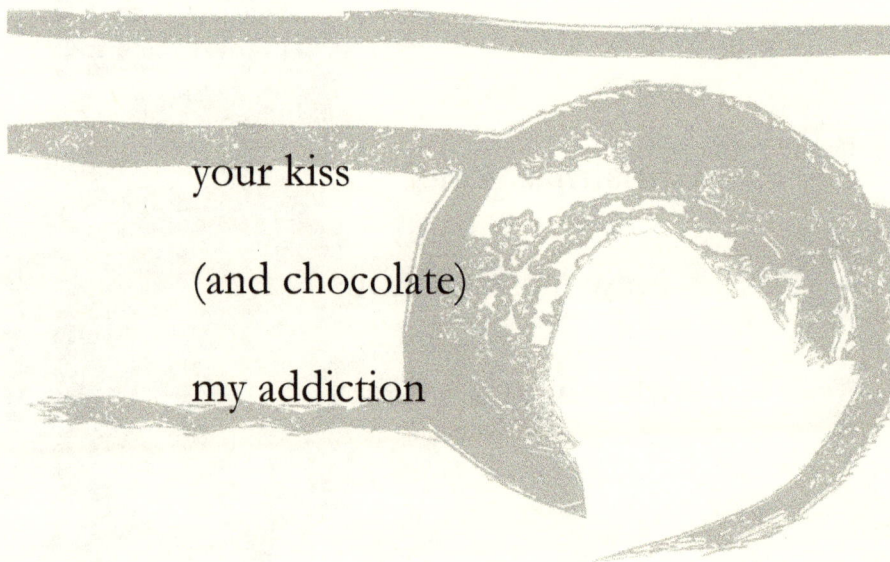

your kiss

(and chocolate)

my addiction

the embrace of a friend

kiss of heart's true love

I can do naught but cherish

low autumn sun

illuminates your face-

radiant smile

following my heart

never easy-

like herding cats

sapphire sky morning-

midsummer sunlight

illuminates a path to your heart

kisses via text–

an instant message

hinting at those L words

illuminated by Christmas light

your face – lips – kiss

beyond temptation

like a magpie

you have stolen my heart

making it shine all the brighter

seeing her was sweet–

kissing her was sweeter

for I could taste her heart

your hand in mine

warm against Winter's chill-

this season's love

stolen moments together

shine all the more

in my greedy eyes

birthday girl wrapped

in a duvet-

a gift to be opened?

a taste of you

- my forbidden fruit -

and I fall

blunt behind clouds

yet Luna still blesses us-

madly in love

reading of impossible feats

marveling at their daring-

I kiss you

black ice under foot-

my head's in the clouds

remembering our Summer

in the night sky

you are my North Star-

a heavenly body

mist shrouded morning

but with you in my minds eye

I can see forever

awakening to your presence

my sleeping sweetheart-

or am I still dreaming?

stretching out his limbs

he awakens renewed-

reborn from pain

feeding my body

as you have fed my soul

only serves to feed my heart

gentle autumn evening-

walking hand in hand

we pause – kiss – and move on

caught up in the crowd-

I look into your eyes

and there is only Us

curled in bed with you

sharing the moment-

eternity in an hour

amid chaotic Christmas consumerism

I take your hand in mine-

a guide through the blizzard of bodies

kissing-distance close

and looking into your eyes

words form on my lips

winter wonderland kiss

with only a robin as our witness-

tell it to the birds and the bees

your slightest touch

my everything-

forever

our friendship-

the stuff of myth

and legend

sunlit Sunday morning stroll-

crisp Winter's day

warmed by your smile

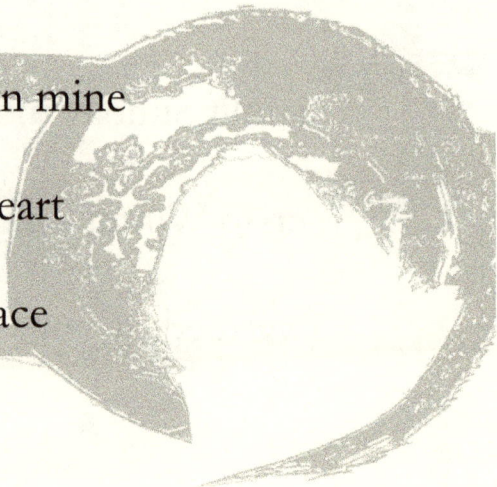

your hand in mine

holds my heart

in an embrace

kissing you breathes life

into my existence

resuscitating my soul

white Winter wonderland

all the brighter

with you in it

I never want to need you

I only ever want to want you—

always

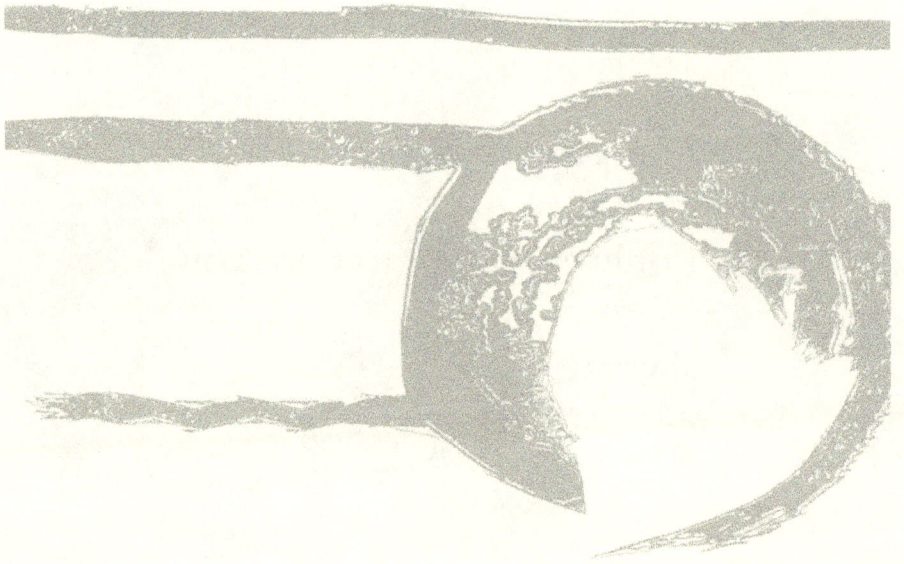

For Gail

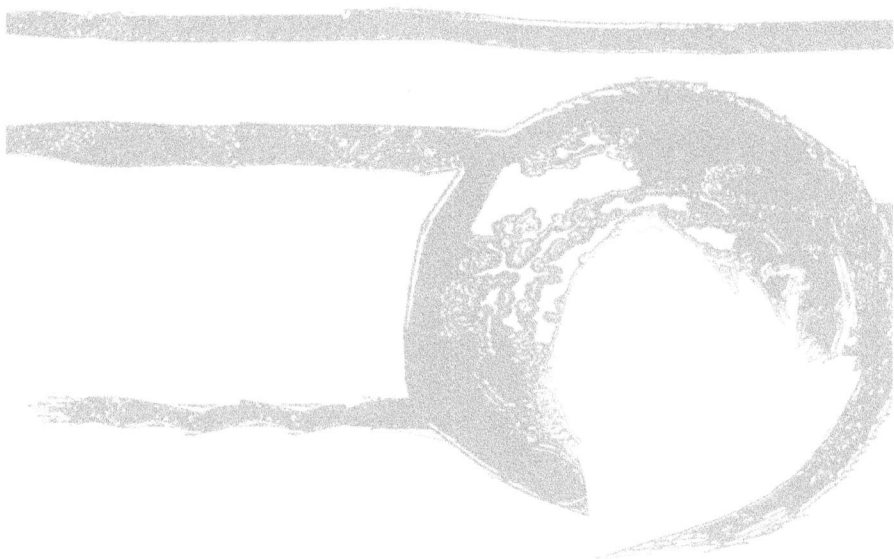

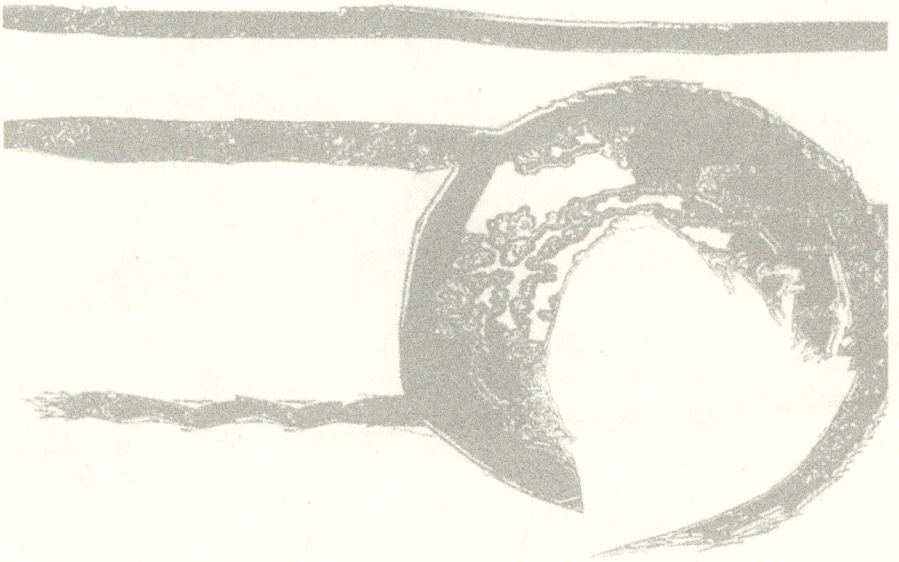